HARALD IN BYZANTIUM

HARALD IN BYZANTIUM

A cycle of poems by
Kevin Crossley-Holland

with illustrations by
Chris Riddell

2022

Published by Arc Publications,
Nanholme Mill, Shaw Wood Road
Todmorden OL14 6DA, UK
www.arcpublications.co.uk

978 1911469 12 4

Design by Tony Ward
Printed in the UK by ImprintDigital.com,
Upton Pyne, Exeter, Devon

ACKNOWLEDGEMENTS

While this cycle was still in the making, earlier versions
of several of these poems were first published in
The Breaking Hour (Enitharmon, 2015).

Arc Chapbook Series
Series Editor: Tony Ward

Harald Hardrada (née Sigurdsson) was the greatest warrior of his age.

He was only fifteen when he fought and was badly wounded at the battle of Stiklestad (1030). During the following fifteen years he served first as a young mercenary in Russia before joining the Varangian guard, the crack regiment who guarded the Emperors of Byzantium. He fought in Sicily and the Balkans and Asia Minor to preserve the porous Empire, escorted members of the royal family to Jerusalem, and won immense wealth, before returning in 1045 to Norway with his banner, Land-Waster, to contest and win the crown. He was killed in battle at Stamford Bridge in 1066.

Harald was a man of ferocious energy, burning ambition, and a sense of destiny, with an imposing physical appearance (he had a blonde beard and floppy moustache, one eyebrow was higher than the other, and he was 'a full hand's height taller than other men'). But for all his innate gifts, he had to learn how to be a leader, to understand how politics was largely a matter of attending to personal relationships, and to grasp matters of precedence and status. His defects, moreover, were scarcely fewer than his skills. He was cunning and cruel and vengeful.

Unsurprisingly, Harald was hugely attractive to women. The elderly Empress Zoe unsuccessfully tried to take him to bed; he had a clandestine and passionate affair with her niece, Maria; and Harald's Saga tells us how other well-born women risked life and limb to spring him out of prison…

The cycle consists of short poems in the persona of Harald during his formative years in Byzantium. Passionate and decided, fierce and terse and I hope sometimes witty, they're not narratives but revelations, turning on Harald's engagement with warfare, leadership, love and the contrasts between the appearance and values of the glittering hard-edged northern world, still half in thrall to the old Norse gods, and the softer, more seductive south.

Above all, they're the words of a young man amongst men (most of them blue-eyed and tattooed) whose lives are in his hands, and on whom his own success and fame depend.

Kevin Crossley-Holland

1

When I was a boy, I was a boy.
I wrestled with my brothers
and made myself sick on all
the blueberries we picked. I flew kites.

It was those blades at Stiklestad
cut my childhood out of me.

There's a poem about how fate can finish off
anyone, even an unfated man,
if his bravery is wanting.
His bravery, but also his discipline.
If one man breaks the shield-rampart
all his companions suffer.

Each of us could do with a magic reindeer coat
purchased at some extortionate price
but life's not like that, there's no easy way out.

My men here understand this.
They know the watchwords:
forethought, caution, action, effect.
I'll brook no disobedience. None at all.

2

At Stiklestad I was fifteen
and still too eager. An older man
saved me from myself

when that Swede's spear
opened my entrails. Then his family
hid me all winter, and they fed me.

Promises come cheap; honouring them seldom.
But he kept his word. At my bidding
he sailed south, and fought with me in Sicily.

Each of us needs around us not only
young men but those who knew us young.
Home in Trondheim, I'll seek him out again.

3

Garthar, Garthar, not here,
not there, but in between.

In her forests she will grant you
nothing but nettles, thorns, teeth,
night eyes shining. There's no escape.

Her hair, wild black, a dozen times
she winds it around you...

*

But at Bosphorus, they welcomed my dragon-prow,
waving from their swarm of dugouts
or cobles or knars or whatever they call them.

Sails blue as promises, pink as flamingos
and green and bitter as kelp.

I was not born yesterday.
Sweet today is often sour tomorrow.

My fjord winds to a turf-roof
and the glacier's blue teeth.
I can hear the quernstone
grinding the salt in the northern sea.

Your smooth-skinned channel slides
between bluffs. Even when the water
is pink, violet, you can see her depths,
her rounded white rocks shimmering.
I do not know where you are taking me
but I have no choice, only an imperative.

The eyes of my women
are dawn-grey, dawn-blue.
Here, they are black stars,

and a little painted fingernail
achieves more than a northern
screech or pitchfork.

In a climate cold and wet
there's very little blaze,
not even much smoulder.

I have resolved to stay
in Miklagard a little longer.

Three Anglians have arrived at court.
Thorold understands their muddy tongue
and says they come from Jorvik.

They tell him they're pilgrims
suffering for love of the White Christ,
journeying they care not where.
Oh?

To have travelled so far
not as traders, missionaries or messengers
means only they had much to get away from:
not just some debt or a furious woman;
their own death-shadows, no doubt.

They've told Thorold they're ready
to serve the Empress –
but in this benighted place
a dozen counsellors are arguing
about whether to trust and enlist them,
and if not, whether...

Either they'll be sent packing
or I'll be detailed
to take care of them
like those Burgundians.

One of them reminds me of Guttorm,
my half-brother.

This week another boatload of young bucks sailed in,
their mouth stuffed with oaths,
and, as usual, they know all the answers.

This tide of refugees, for instance
– more, many more than shoals of herring in the fjord.

It's better to go for the jugular, is it,
better to stem the tide at source?
Yes, commit all us Varangians to an invasion.
No, better to meet them at the crossing-places
and cut off their right hands
and send them home.

Well then, extend our borders...
As if this Empire's not already bulbous and porous.
And who would govern the governors?

Ah! Here's a thinker.
Better long words than actions, he advocates.
Better persuasion then incursion.
Have these refugees grasp that our welcome
will be strictly conditional – they'll be un-citizens
– arse-lickers, and slaves.

And this one is a bloody missionary... Ye gods!
Do you really believe that if we baptise them
they'll troop back to Jerusalem?
Have you the least idea what they're fleeing from?
Have you never heard of the power of dreams?

I've served here for nine half-years.
There cannot be a single strategy,
there can be no checkmate.
The next right choice
is all we can play for.

I've been told
half-a-dozen of my men
have been bad-mouthing me
since we set foot in Sicily.

That one,
and the one from Kiev over there….
I know their names.

Pretending they mean to murder me
tonight in my own tent,
my faithful two body-men
will approach them
to enlist their support,

and if any of them agree
I'll have them hanged in the morning.
Breakfast for buzzards.

After that, I'll call for new oaths.
I serve the Empress,
and each Varangian here serves me.

'Chickens! Harald, don't waste your time on them.
And that includes your elder brothers.'

I was three when I pulled the king's beard
and he laughed, but his pupils were black pinpricks.

No one can accuse that fucking Turk
of being quick-witted, let alone witty,
and the way he squawks at me
curdles my cheeks. But he's wily and stubborn,
and in the name of our common cause, Holy Empire,
I'll do well to study his tactics
and how to proceed against him.

Trapped in the mixing-bowl of some hill-troll.
Scorching wind from Africa… red dust whirling
round me, red dust in my throat, my gut.
Then a raven flops down and one-eyes me.

'Red dust? No, not only. Harald, you are blood.
You are memory. That stained field…
Wherever you are, whoever your enemy,
when you raise your right arm, strike for me.'

Grasses soon grow on a little-trodden road
but leader and led can never rub shoulders.
That's the cost. Have it said
Harald always understood that of all gifts
friendship freely-given is the greatest.

*

No blood-friend tells you
only what you want to hear.

You can add that truth to Havamal.
And here's another:

Self-love is sponge.
Self-respect is forged.

Slingstones have their limitations.
With my battering-ram I'll breach
their soaring walls. And I will dispose
of Gyrgir, that Armenian lout…
I will do this, I will do that,
and that and that. But who can say
whether you will lie with me again,
shining in your cocoon of Jewish silks?

The delicate contraption of your right ankle,
the downy crooks of your arms,
your swan-neck.

They give me back
my elbows and knees, the plates
of my shoulder-bones, the thud,
thud of my heart.

Dear Gods,
I who will rule
the whole northern world. . .
My head is thumping. My heart spinning.

14

I become breathless. I am tormented.
I would trade days
to feel again on my palms
the weight of your perfect breasts,
to hear once more the way
you sweet-mouthed my name.

Let the gods grow old.
Let them become mumbling imbeciles.
Let them become incontinent.

Grant me one night
in your apple-garden
forever young,

and I will outgod the gods.

Many times I've slept under this rough canvas
– my men hawking and swearing all around me –
and often enough I've choked on stinking scat,
listened to hooting owls and slept beneath stars,
all too often wrapped in my own arms.

A spice-trader from Split asked me last week:
'Where you come from? Where you going?'
Each question invites the next: 'What is home?'

Rót… skát… traust…
I like the t… t of the Icelanders,
Distinct, and light as a bleb.
Charming as a scamp's tip-tilted nose.
t… t… still hanging in mid-air
after its word has disappeared.

Our rosy-cheeked Empress, Princess of Peace…
    Purple-pouched, more like.
Silence! Who said that?
    Ghastly hag. Old tombstone.
    Murderous Pumpkin.
Shut your traps or I'll slice
your tongues, I'll tattoo your testicles.
Some men close to our Empress,
our Princess of Peace, have put it about
she's scoffing at me, and says
I'm nothing but the young son of some troll.
    You are, Harald! Harald, you are!
    That harridan, she's jealous.
    She's purple and fifty-four!
Silence!

Mermaids?
A mixed blessing! I've met several.

That moon-mermaid in Syria
on my way back from Jerusalem:
every man and woman worshipped her
although she was made of marble.

As a young boy
I was overwintering in Unst
– a miserable settlement if ever there was –
when a fisherman was trapped by a mermaid's song.
She tried to drown him
but his companions stoned her, and drove her off.

One of my men asserts
a good many of the Irish are descended
from mermaids.

When I'm king I'll tether one
in a pool brimming with saltwater
– also a siren.
They can sing together.

Wise men will teach them our tongue
and ask them all they know
about healing and snaring and underwater,
and what stories they've heard
concerning Aegir and Ran.

I woke from a dream
of my mother's first home on the fiord.

The men greeted me, but not as one of their own.
A stranger was perching in that seat
Thorgeir forged for my mother
from iron bars and little strips.
Then I saw him at the far end of the staithe.
I'd know his wading walk anywhere,
but he was less certain. Knees buckling.

I can go no further. Not one step.
First I have to come back.
That's what I told him.
'You understand that?'

No morning for leaning
into the wind, shadow ribs swept through us.
The water was uneasy, and the islet winked.

'The old are often wise,' he said.
'They may hang with the hides
and flap with the pelts
and rock with the guts in the wind,
but shrivelled skins often give wise advice.
Aegir will smooth your sea-path,' he told me.
'Allfather will fate you to come home.'

'Thorgeir? Deaf as a door-stopper
for the last seven years.'
So said the men.

What was it my English scop sang?
'Amber and jet. Pearl, swansdown.
Woodsmoke, tart and sweet. Sopping
clouds, old habits. Dear unknowings.'

Yes, where's the true tip of the spear
when grapes and figs grow on the terrace?
Men here are pampered and impenitent.
Uncertainty, that's the best mulch.

I ask not for sight but to learn how to see.
Give me high latitudes to grow spirit-fruit.

22

Halfway up, my guide paused
beside a glittering stream and his little daughter
waded in and picked up white pebbles.
This source, he said to me in his laughable Norse,
gallops north. He opened his pale palms.
Novgorod. Ladoga. Baltic.

Unaware of his insolence, he reached up
and tried to put an arm around my shoulders.
I shook it off.

Over there, he said, pointing to a ridge
no more than a shout away,
that source south. Black Sea. Miklagard.

Time was, I didn't hesitate,
not for one moment.
So eager, so full-blooded.
Was my heart that wild?
That unbridled?

Time is, I've got my eye on Time
and what survives it: followers,
the golden crown, hard-edged fame.

Tomorrow, I'll make my peace with Jaroslav
and ask again for the hand of his bracelet-goddess.
I'll point my black prow north.

The old scalds shared what they knew
but it isn't true, not half of it

though half my men swallow it.
They've crossed deep waters
and still think like children.

We see only shadows of the gods,
and they've very little interest in us.
What they're said to have said
is only what we wish they'd say.

But there's one...
In my dreams I often see you
standing in the shade.

Not Frigg, giver of flax, not Fulla,
not even one of the holy thirteen.

But I have always known you,
and now I need you.
Tell me your true name.

I am become like a bottle in the smoke.
If I can trust my translator,
that's what one psalmist sings.
But what's the point of unmanning ourselves,
and declaring our weaknesses?
Many a lad has lived too long
under his father's thumb, and many
haven't mastered how to hoist a sail.
Because of some fool, good plans
have been misunderstood or else stillborn…
No! give me a lump of gammelost
with the tang of mouldering Vikings,
give me fire from a bottle to wash it down.
I'll be true to those who follow me
in the names of firebrands before me.
Let me be blood and flames.

KEVIN CROSSLEY-HOLLAND has had a lifelong interest in Viking literature and history, and is the author of *The Penguin Book of Norse Myths*, as well as translator of *Beowulf* and a Carnegie Medal-winning author for children. He joined forces with Chris Riddell to write / illustrate *Arthur, the Always King* (2021), and his most recent collection of poems, *Gravity for Beginners*, was published by Arc Publications in spring 2021.

CHRIS RIDDELL OBE has won many illustration awards including the UNESCO Prize, the Greenaway Medal (on three occasions) and the Hay Festival Medal for Illustration. As an author his work includes the highly-acclaimed *Ottoline* titles and the 2013 Costa Children's Book Award-winning *Goth Girl* and the *Ghost of a Mouse*, and he has collaborated as an illustrator with Neil Gaiman, the comedian Russell Brand and others. He is passionate about poetry and has curated two anthologies. Chris is also a renowned political cartoonist whose work appears in *The Observer*, the *Literary Review* and the *New Statesman*.

He is a past president of the Schools Library Association, and an ambassador for Booktrust and Amnesty International.